Contents

What Became of Them?

He was a rat, and she was a rat,
And down in one hole they did dwell,
And both were as black as a witch's cat,
And they loved one another well.

He had a tail, and she had a tail,
Both long and curling and fine;
And each said, "Yours is the finest tail
In the world, excepting mine."

He smelt the cheese, and she smelt the cheese,
And they both pronounced it good;
And both remarked it would greatly add
To the charms of their daily food.

First published in 2010 by Miles Kelly Publishing Ltd
Harding's Barn, Bardfield End Green, Thaxted, Essex, CM6 3PX, UK

2 4 6 8 10 9 7 5 3 1

Editorial Director Belinda Gallagher

Art Director Jo Cowan

Assistant Editor Claire Philip

Designer Joe Jones

Junior Designer Kayleigh Allen

Production Manager Elizabeth Collins

Reprographics Stephan Davis, Ian Paulyn

ISBN 978-1-84810-373-3

Printed in China

British Library Cataloguing-in-Publication Data
A catalogue record for this book is available from the British Library

ACKNOWLEDGEMENTS

The publishers would like to thank Kirsten Wilson for
the illustrations she contributed to this book.

All other artwork from the Miles Kelly Artwork Bank

The publishers would like to thank iStockphoto.com for the use
of their photographs on pages 18 (mcswin) and 34 (Elena Kalistratova)

Made with paper from a sustainable forest

www.mileskelly.net
info@mileskelly.net

www.factsforprojects.com

Self-publish your
children's book

buddingpress.co.uk

So he ventured out, and she ventured out,
And I saw them go with pain;
But what befell them I never can tell,
For they never came back again.

Anonymous

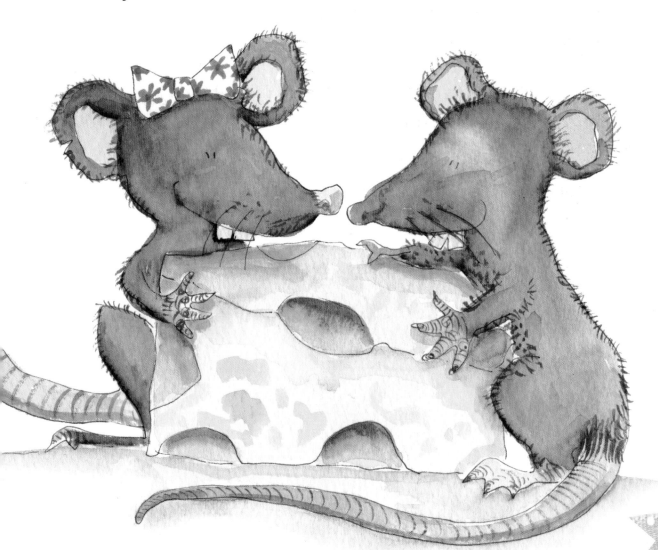

A Cat Came Fiddling

A cat came fiddling out of a barn,
With a pair of bagpipes under her arm.
She could sing nothing but fiddle dee dee,
The mouse has married the bumblebee.
Pipe, cat; dance, mouse,
We'll have a wedding at our good house.

Anonymous

The Little Turtle

There was a little turtle.
He lived in a box.
He swam in a puddle.
He climbed on the rocks.

He snapped at a mosquito.
He snapped at a flea.
He snapped at a minnow.
And he snapped at me.

He caught the mosquito.
He caught the flea.
He caught the minnow.
But he didn't catch me.

Vachel Lindsay

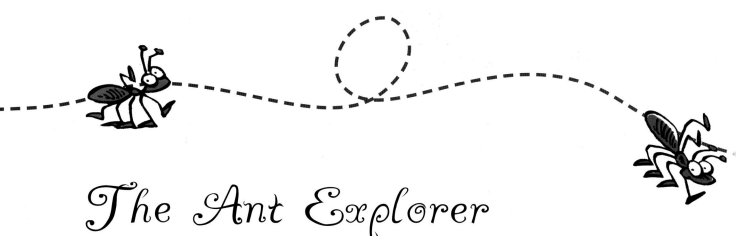

The Ant Explorer

Once a little sugar ant made up his mind to roam —
To far away far away, far away from home.
He had eaten all his breakfast, and he had his ma's consent
To see what he should chance to see and here's the way he went —
Up and down a fern frond, round and round a stone,
Down a gloomy gully, where he loathed to be alone,
Up a mighty mountain range, seven inches high,
Through the fearful forest grass that nearly hid the sky,
Out along a bracken bridge, bending in the moss,
Till he reached a dreadful desert that was feet and feet across.

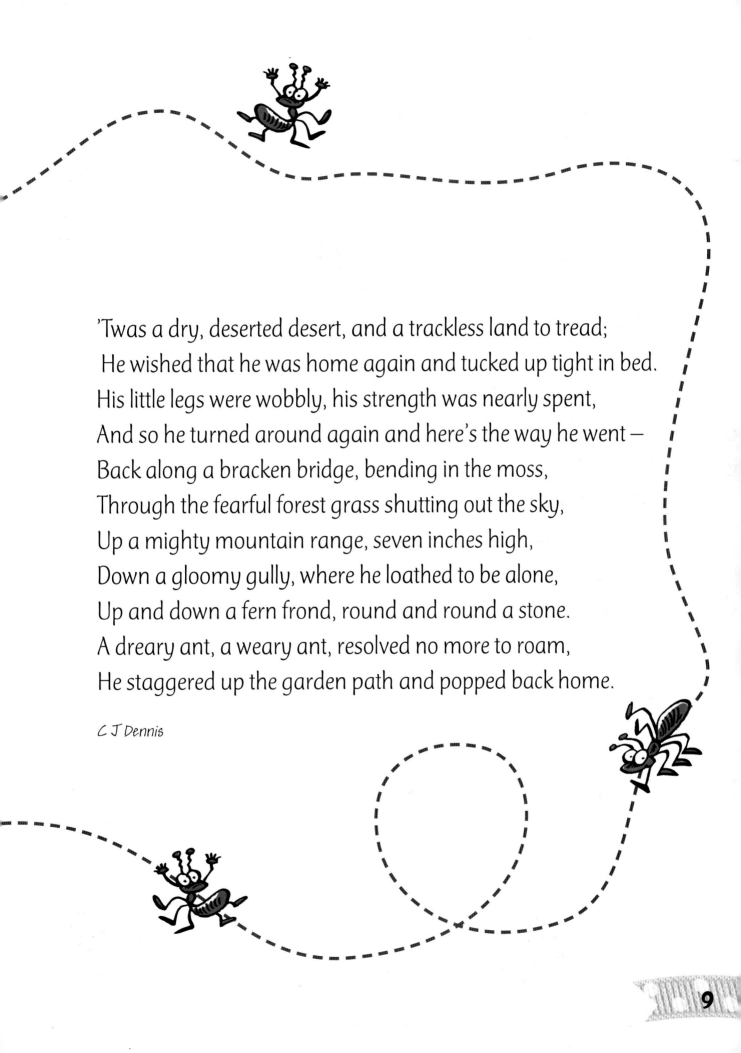

'Twas a dry, deserted desert, and a trackless land to tread;
 He wished that he was home again and tucked up tight in bed.
His little legs were wobbly, his strength was nearly spent,
And so he turned around again and here's the way he went —
Back along a bracken bridge, bending in the moss,
Through the fearful forest grass shutting out the sky,
Up a mighty mountain range, seven inches high,
Down a gloomy gully, where he loathed to be alone,
Up and down a fern frond, round and round a stone.
A dreary ant, a weary ant, resolved no more to roam,
He staggered up the garden path and popped back home.

C J Dennis

The Fox

The Fox went out one winter night,
And prayed the moon to give him light,
For he'd many a mile to go that night,
Before he reached his den, O!
Den, O! Den, O!
For he'd many a mile to go that night,
For he'd many a mile to go that night,
Before he reached his den, O!

At last he came to a farmer's yard,
Where the ducks and the geese were all afear'd
"The best of you all shall grease my beard,
Before I leave the Town O!
Town O! Town O!
The best of you all shall grease my beard,
The best of you all shall grease my beard,
Before I leave the Town O!

He took the grey goose by the neck,
He laid a duck across his back,
And heeded not their quack! quack! quack!
The legs of all dangling down, O!
Down, O! Down O!
And heeded not their quack! quack! quack!
And heeded not their quack! quack! quack!
The legs of all dangling down, O!

Then old mother Slipper Slopper jump'd out of bed
And out of the window she pop't her head,
Crying "Oh! John, John! the grey goose is dead,
And the fox is over the down, O!"
Down, O! Down O!
Crying "Oh! John, John! the grey goose is dead,
Crying "Oh! John, John! the grey goose is dead,
And the fox is over the down, O!"

Then John got up to the top
    o' the hill,
And blew this horn both loud
    and shrill,
"Blow on" said Reynard,
    "your music still,
Whilst I trot home to my den, O",
Den, O! Den, O!,
"Blow on" said Reynard, "your
    music still,
"Blow on" said Reynard, "your music still,
Whilst I trot home to my den, O",

12

At last he came to his cosy den,
Where sat his young ones, nine or ten,
Quoth they, "Daddy, you must go there again,
For sure, 'tis a lucky town, O!"
Town, O! Town, O!
Quoth they, "Daddy, you must go there again,
Quoth they, "Daddy, you must go there again,
    For sure, 'tis a lucky town, O!"

    The fox and wife without any strife,
      They cut up the goose without fork or knife,
      And said 'twas the best they had eat in their life,
      And the young ones pick'd the bones, O!
    Bones, O! Bones, O!
   And said 'twas the best they had eat in their life,
   And said 'twas the best they had eat in their life,
   And the young ones pick'd the bones, O!

Anonymous

Kitten's Complaint

In Winter when the air is chill,
And winds are blowing loud and shrill,
All snug and warm I sit and purr,
Wrapped in my overcoat of fur.
In Summer quite the other way,
I find it very hot all day,
But Human People do not care,
For they have nice thin clothes to wear.
And does it not seem hard to you,
When all the world is like a stew,
And I am much too warm to purr,
I have to wear my Winter Fur?

Oliver Herford

Commissariat Camels

We haven't a camelty tune of our own
To help us trollop along,
But every neck is a hair-trombone
(Rtt-ta-ta-ta! is a hair-trombone!)
And this is our marching-song:

Can't! Don't! Shan't! Won't!

Pass it along the line!
Somebody's pack has slid from his back,
Wish it were only mine!
Somebody's load has tipped off in the road –
Cheer for a halt and a row!

Urrr! Yarrh! Grr! Arrh!

Somebody's catching it now!

Rudyard Kipling

Commissariat a system for supplying an army with food

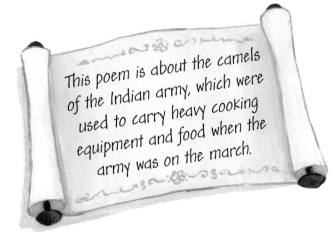

This poem is about the camels of the Indian army, which were used to carry heavy cooking equipment and food when the army was on the march.

From **Dog**

O little friend, your nose is ready; you sniff,
Asking for that expected walk,
(Your nostrils full of the happy rabbit-whiff)
And almost talk. . .

Out through the garden your head is already low.
You are going your walk, you know,
And your limbs will draw
Joy from the earth through the touch of your padded paw. . .

Home. . . and further joy will be waiting there:
Supper full of the taste of bone.
You lift up your nose again, and
　　sniff, and stare
For the rapture known

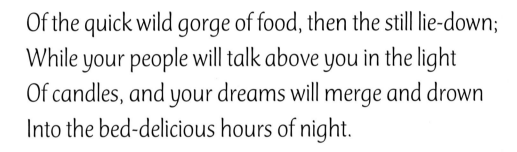

Of the quick wild gorge of food, then the still lie-down;
While your people will talk above you in the light
Of candles, and your dreams will merge and drown
Into the bed-delicious hours of night.

Harold Monro

What is Pink?

What is pink? A rose is pink
By the fountain's brink.
What is red? A poppy's red
In its barley bed.
What is blue? The sky is blue
Where the clouds float through.
What is white? A swan is white
Sailing in the light.
What is yellow? Pears are yellow,
Rich and ripe and mellow.
What is green? The grass is green,
With small flowers between.
What is violet? Clouds are violet
In the summer twilight.
What is orange? Why, an orange,
Just an orange!

Christina Rossetti

From To a Butterfly

Oh! Pleasant, pleasant were the days,

The time, when, in our childish plays,

My sister Emmeline and I

Together chased the butterfly!

A very hunter did I rush

Upon the prey – with leaps and springs

I followed on from brake to bush;

But she, God love her, feared to brush

The dust from off its wings.

William Wordsworth

Brake a small clump of trees

Milk for the Cat

When the tea is brought at five o'clock,
And all the neat curtains are drawn with care,
The little black cat with bright green eyes
Is suddenly purring there.
At first she pretends, having nothing to do,
She has come in merely to blink by the grate,
But, though tea may be late or the milk may be sour,
She is never late.
And presently her agate eyes
Take a soft large milky haze,
And her independent casual glance
Becomes a stiff, hard gaze.
Then she stamps her claws or
    lifts her ears,
Or twists her tail and begins
    to stir,
Till suddenly all her lithe
    body becomes
One breathing, trembling purr.

The children eat and wriggle and laugh;
The two old ladies stroke their silk:
But the cat is grown small and thin with desire,
Transformed to a creeping lust for milk.
The white saucer like some full moon descends
At last from the clouds of the table above;
She sighs and dreams and thrills and glows,
Transfigured with love.

She nestles over the shining rim,
Buries her chin in the creamy sea;
Her tail hangs loose; each drowsy paw
Is doubled under each bending knee.
A long, dim ecstasy holds her life;
Her world is an infinite shapeless white,
Till her tongue has curled the last holy drop,
Then she sinks back into the night,
Draws and dips her body to heap
Her sleepy nerves in the great arm-chair,
Lies defeated and buried deep
Three or four hours unconscious there.

Harold Monro

Dapple-Grey

I had a little pony,
His name was Dapple-Grey,
I lent him to a lady,
To ride a mile away.
She whipped him, she slashed him,
She rode him through the mire;
I would not lend my pony now
For all the lady's hire.

Anonymous

Donkey

If I had a donkey that wouldn't go,
Would I beat him? Oh, no, no.
I'd put him in the barn and give
   him some corn.
The best little donkey that ever
   was born.

Anonymous

The Flowers

All the names I know from nurse:
Gardener's garters, Shepherd's purse,
Bachelor's buttons, Lady's smock,
And the Lady Hollyhock.

Fairy places, fairy things,
Fairy woods where the wild bee wings,
Tiny trees for tiny dames,
These must all be fairy names!

Tiny woods below whose boughs
Shady fairies weave a house;
Tiny tree-tops, rose or thyme,
Where the braver fairies climb!

Fair are grown-up people's trees,
But the fairest woods are these;
Where, if I were not so tall,
I should live for good and all.

Robert Louis Stevenson

Squirrel

Whisky Frisky,
Hippity hop,
Up he goes
To the tree-top!

Whirly, twirly,
Round and round,
Down he scampers
To the ground.

Furly, curly,
What a tail!
Tall as a feather,
Broad as a sail!

Where's his supper?
In the shell,
Snappy, cracky,
Out it fell!

Anonymous

To a Squirrel at Kyle-Na-No

Come play with me;
Why should you run
Through the shaking tree
As though I'd a gun
To strike you dead?
When all I would do
Is to scratch your head
And let you go.

W B Yeats

Robin Redbreast

Goodbye, goodbye to Summer!
For Summer's nearly done;
The garden smiling faintly,
Cool breezes in the sun;
Our Thrushes now are silent,
Our Swallows flown away –
Hang russet on the bough,
It's Autumn, Autumn, Autumn late,
'Twill soon be winter now.
Robin, Robin Redbreast,
O Robin dear!

And what will this poor Robin do?
For pinching days are near.

The fireside for the Cricket,
The wheatsack for the Mouse,
When trembling night-winds whistle
And moan all round the house;
The frosty ways like iron,
The branches plumed with snow –
Alas! In Winter, dead, and dark,
Where can poor Robin go?
Robin, Robin Redbreast,
O Robin dear!
And a crumb of bread for Robin,
His little heart to cheer.

William Allingham

Jabberwocky

'Twas brillig, and the slithy toves
Did gyre and gimble in the wabe;
All mimsy were the borogoves,
And the mome raths outgrabe.

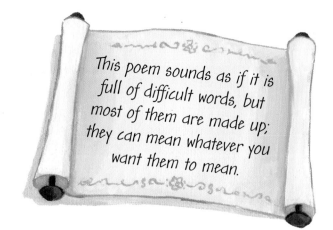

This poem sounds as if it is full of difficult words, but most of them are made up; they can mean whatever you want them to mean.

"Beware the Jabberwock, my son!
The jaws that bite, the claws that catch!
Beware the Jubjub bird, and shun
The frumious Bandersnatch!"

He took his vorpal sword in hand:
Long time the manxome foe he sought.
So rested he by the Tumtum tree,
And stood awhile in thought.

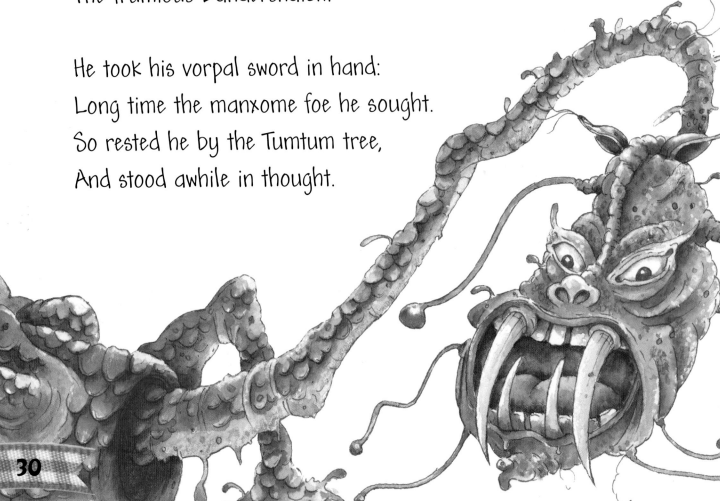

And as in uffish thought he stood,
The Jabberwock with eyes of flame,
Came whiffling through the tulgey wood,
And burbled as it came!

One, two! One, two! And through, and through
The vorpal blade went snicker-snack!
He left it dead, and with its head
He went galumphing back.

"And hast thou slain the Jabberwock?
    Come to my arms, my beamish boy!
        Oh, frabjous day! Callooh! Callay!"
        He chortled in his joy.

'Twas brillig, and the slithy toves
Did gyre and gimble in the wabe;
All mimsy were the borogoves
And the mome raths outgrabe.

Lewis Carroll

The Camel's Complaint

Canary-birds feed on sugar and seed,
Parrots have crackers to crunch;
And, as for the poodles, they tell me the noodles
Have chickens and cream for their lunch.
But there's never a question
About **MY** digestion –
ANYTHING does for me!

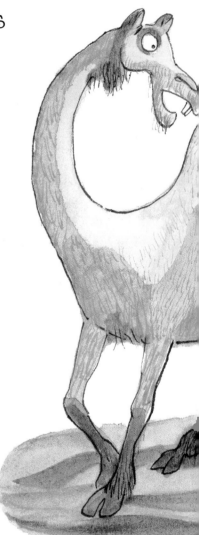

Cats, you're aware, can repose in a chair,
Chickens can roost upon rails;
Puppies are able to sleep in a stable,
And oysters can slumber in pails.
But no one supposes a poor camel dozes –
ANY PLACE does for me!

Lambs are enclosed where it's never exposed,
Coops are constructed for hens;
Kittens are treated to houses well-heated,
And pigs are protected by pens.

But a Camel comes handy
Wherever it's sandy –
ANYWHERE does for me!

People would laugh if you rode a giraffe,
Or mounted the back of an ox;
It's nobody's habit to ride on a rabbit,
Or try to bestraddle a fox.
But as for a Camel, he's
Ridden by families –
ANY LOAD does for me!

A snake is as round as a hole in the ground,
And weasels are wavy and sleek;
And no alligator could ever be straighter
Than lizards that live in a creek.
But a Camel's all lumpy
And bumpy and humpy –
ANY SHAPE does for me!

Charles E Carryl

The Little Ladybird

Ladybird, ladybird! Fly away home!
The field-mouse has gone to her nest,
The daisies have shut up their sleepy red eyes,
And the bees and the birds are at rest.
Ladybird, ladybird! Fly away home!
The glow-worm is lighting her lamp,
The dew's falling fast, and your fine speckled wings
Will flag with the close-clinging damp.
Ladybird, ladybird! Fly away home!
Good luck if you reach it at last!
The owl's come abroad, and the bat's on the roam,
Sharp set from their Ramazan fast.

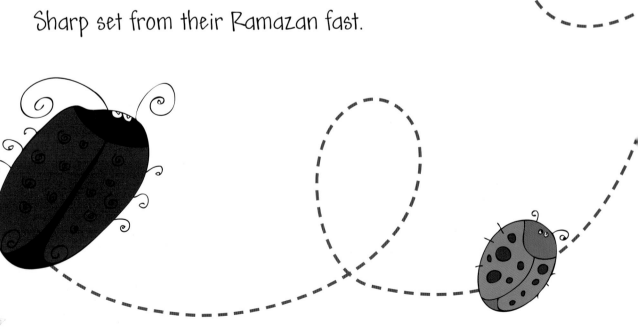

Ladybird, ladybird! Fly away home!
The fairy bells tinkle afar!
Make haste or they'll catch you, and harness you fast
With a cobweb to Oberon's car.
Ladybird, ladybird! Fly away home!
To your house in the old willow-tree,
Where your children so dear have invited the ant
And a few cosy neighbours to tea.
Ladybird, ladybird! Fly away home!
And if not gobbled up by the way,
Nor yoked by the fairies to Oberon's car,
You're in luck! and that's all I've to say.

Caroline Southey

Oberon the king of the fairies
Ramazan early spelling of
Ramadan, the Islamic festival
where most people fast (don't
eat until the evening)

An Autumn Greeting

"Come, little leaves,"
Said the wind one day,
"Come over the meadows
With me, and play;
Put on your dresses
Of red and gold;
Summer is gone,
And the days grow cold."

Soon as the leaves
Heard the wind's loud call,
Down they came fluttering,
One and all;
Over the meadows
They danced and flew,
Singing the soft
Little songs they knew.

Dancing and flying
The little leaves went;
Winter had called them
And they were content –
Soon fast asleep
In their earthy beds,
The snow laid a soft mantle
Over their heads.

George Cooper

Bedtime in Summer

In winter I get up at night
And dress by yellow candle-light.
In summer quite the other way,
I have to go to bed by day.
I have to go to bed and see
The birds still hopping on the tree,
Or hear the grown-up people's feet
Still going past me in the street.
And does it not seem hard to you,
When all the sky is clear and blue,
And I should like so much to play,
To have to go to bed by day?

Robert Louis Stevenson

Young Night-thought

All night long and every night,
When my mama puts out the light,
I see the people marching by,
As plain as day before my eye.
Armies and emperor and kings,
All carrying different kinds of things,
And marching in so grand a way,
You never saw the like by day.
So fine a show was never seen
At the great circus on the green;
For every kind of beast and man
Is marching in that caravan.
As first they move a little slow,
But still the faster on they go,
And still beside me close I keep
Until we reach the town of Sleep.

Robert Louis Stevenson

Index of First Lines